How a Smart Watch Saved My Life

Sarah McPherson

Copyright © 2024 by Sarah McPherson

ISBN – 978-0-6457533-9-4

All rights reserved.

No portion of this book may be reproduced in any form without written permission from the publisher or author.

This publication is designed to provide accurate and authoritative information in regard to the subject matter covered. It is sold with the understanding that neither the author nor the publisher is engaged in rendering legal, investment, accounting or other professional services. While the publisher and author have used their best efforts in preparing this book, they make no representations or warranties with respect to the accuracy or completeness of the contents of this book and specifically disclaim any implied warranties of merchantability or fitness for a particular purpose. No warranty may be created or extended by sales representatives or written sales materials. The advice and strategies contained herein may not be suitable for your situation. You should consult with a professional when appropriate. Neither the publisher nor the author shall be liable for any loss of profit or any other commercial damages, including but not limited to special, incidental, consequential, personal, or other damages.

Contents

Dedication	VI
1. Heart	1
2. My greatest gift	5
3. 1st April 2020	15
4. Wife, Mother, Twin.	23
5. My life.	35
6. August 2020	45
7. November 13th - 16th 2020	55
8. 10th December 2020	61

9.	12th January 2021	67
10.	Moving Home	75
11.	The question of Resilence.	81
12.	The world turned upside down	89
13.	The Diagnosis	95
14.	9th March 2021	99
15.	One night	107
16.	April 2021	115
17.	14th June 2021	121
18.	Fear	129
19.	March 2022	135
20.	A reminder	141
21.	13th September 2022	147
22.	Another Journey	157
23.	Follow up	161
24.	Being thankful	167
25.	28th August 2023	171

26.	August 2024	177
27.	Facing your mortality	183
28.	The Journey	189
	Thanks for Reading!	193

To Scott,

You saved my life, you are my everything.

To Bek,

Thanks for always being their for me, as I look back on my life I am so glad to have you as my twin sister.

To Dr Chee,

With your skilled hands and unwavering expertise, you gave me a second chance at life.

Heart

8th February 2021

I felt my heartbeat quicken as I sat in the doctor's office, ironic since the reason I was sitting there in the first place was my heart rate was low, dangerously low. Dropping down to 35, sometimes even 30 beats a minute each night as I slept.

But at that moment, in the Cardiologist's office, with my hand gripped tightly in my husband's, it pounded loudly. My Cardiologist began speaking, and everything stopped, except that loud rhythmic beating of my heart in my chest. I heard him speak, but everything inside me went numb.

"Without this operation, you have 3 years left. He paused, looking back it felt like it was for effect, although I know he was just clearing his throat. "Five, if you are lucky, now we can try medication, but I am concerned, the medication will lower your blood pressure and heart rate even further, and they are both already too low."

I blinked, and my mind began racing, trying to keep up with the words.

"The Operation isn't without risks...."

The words continued but time stood still. It felt like a movie, his voice whilst still at the same volume, became distant, muffled even, as the gravity of his words hit me. This couldn't be, I was only in my 30's I had four kids, and they needed me, I looked over at my husband. He needed me. I had no choice.

"Do the operation", I said without hesitation, my voice sounding calmer than I felt.

I looked over the shock firmly in my husband's eyes, the weight of this news was like a cloud that had descended on him.

"When?" I asked

"Four weeks" the Cardiologist replied without emotion.

I breathed deep, I had no choice, it had to work.

My Greatest Gift

Not many people can say that they have given someone the ultimate gift. A gift so valuable that the recipient could truly say is priceless. That they have given someone a gift that has truly saved their life. But luckily for me, my husband can.

He purchased something for me, that is the very reason I am still alive today.

I am what you would say an early adopter of technology, even as a 16-year-old I was the first person in my house to get a mobile phone, a gift from my older sister. I loved it. As a teenager, I was very sporty and was out most nights playing some form of sport and my sister thought a phone would be the best way to keep me safe.

She had recently won a sizable sum in a competition from a now-discontinued candy, which allowed her to buy her first car and a special gift for each of her siblings. Growing up without financial security and many times without a car, we relied on public transport and found ourselves in unsafe situations. So, that phone was more than just a device—it was a lifeline, providing me and my twin sister who was often at my side, with security we hadn't felt before.

We didn't have much growing up, Our

clothes were hand-me-downs or from op shops. We didn't have a lot of fancy stuff, our computer a rental that we shared between the 7 of us, but I loved technology, I loved exploring new things. I still remember my favorite thing I owned was a hybrid of an electronic typewriter that my dad had found at a garage sale. I still remember typing a line into the computer, pressing enter then watching it print.

So the moment I got my first Nokia phone I was hooked, from that minute I would become an early adopter of all technologies.

We might not have had much growing up, but what we did have was a strong work ethic.

You see our Dad was a free spirit, he never really grew up, we moved around from school to school, and by the time I was in Grade 6, we had been to 5 schools, more if you count the term we did of homeschooling. My mum juggling trying to teach three young kids, whilst caring for two toddlers, and living with her mother-in-law in a small 3-bedroom house. It wasn't very easy for her, so after a term, we all went back off to school.

We always rented, Dad didn't want to be locked into a house, he liked to move as the whim took him, as well as different houses. Dad's gypsy like lifestyle extended to his work life as well. He had lots of different business ideas. In his mind they were family businesses so that meant his family and his kids worked in them.

My childhood memories, of these businesses are a huge part of my childhood, learning to build fish tanks and feeding animals when he owned Cradle Mountain Aquarium, a homage to Tasmania, one of the many places we had lived. Serving food in a café he ran for a short period on Saturday mornings, collecting cans after speedway racers, selling soft toys, and boxes of nappies at trash and treasure stalls, or sno cone stalls at the big day out and other music festivals. The list was endless, and then the one business that he started when I was only 13 that he continued with until he passed away, a cleaning business in the entertainment industry.

Now work for the family business was not always profitable, but it taught us to work hard so as soon as we were legally allowed to get a job, we did, and with that came a financial freedom that we had never felt before.

It gave me the freedom to save and have our very own things.

Now I have always loved music so when the first iPod came out, I went out and got one, and spent ages choosing hundreds of songs to put on it. This was well before streaming when you had to buy the CDs and transfer the songs onto your iPod. When the iPod mini came out, I got that too, my collection of gadgets was beginning to build up.

When the first Blackberry came out I was so jealous when my sister had one, but it wasn't enough for me to give up my Nokia 5110 and my Snakes game.

But years later when the iPhone came out, I needed one, some might say it was a want, but to me, it was a need. I waited patiently until it was available in Australia and upgraded my phone from my trusty Nokia to the iPhone, and very quickly I was converted. So when I needed a tablet, the iPad made sense.

Next thing came a Mac, I am a keen photographer so a Mac just made sense to me. I am not so sure my husband and kids agreed, as they continue to try and talk me back into Windows computers, but as soon as I needed to upgrade my computer to a laptop, I purchased my Mac.

Like many of us out there Apple had firmly taken over my life.

Our kitchen is full of appliances, from Crepe and waffle makers, Thermomix, and blenders, Our house is full of sound bars, ring lights, and any other gadget that social media seems to sell to me.

So when I heard that Apple had designed a smartwatch, I was fascinated by it. I began to do my research, reading countless articles. Now I hadn't worn a watch in years, but like my house full of gadgets, once I saw it I was intrigued, I knew that an Apple Watch was worth looking into.

I was never one to wear a watch, as a child jewellery was not something we put much value on, I was an active child, more of a tomboy, happily playing outside, and actively playing sports. Jewellery just got in the way, and truth be told I would have probably lost it. Forgetting to take it off before a game.

I had tried to wear watches before and they had never lasted, I vividly remember getting a Mickey Mouse watch as a child and I wore it for a couple of days before I took it off to go swimming and never wore it again.

But now back to my greatest gift, my younger sister came over one day wearing her new Apple Watch, and I grilled her on all the features, I must have made my interest pretty obvious as only a few weeks later, as we wandered into Chadstone, My Husband took me for a walk into the Apple Store, and told me to choose which one I wanted as he was going to buy me one. I was ecstatic, but even in my excitement I would never realize how years later that gift would save my life.

Even as an adult, my jewellery is very sparse,

a simple necklace, a pair of studs, my wedding and engagement ring, and thanks to my husband, an Apple watch.

1st April 2020

Up until April 2020, I can honestly say that I had never experienced the flu. There were times I had been unwell with a cold and had thought that I had the flu, but April 2020 was different.

It was as sudden as it was brutal, with an intensity I wasn't ready for. I woke up one morning and felt like I had just done a huge workout in the gym, every muscle ached, my chest tight, and each time I attempted to breathe it would take my breath away leaving me coughing and gasping for air.

Now, if you ask anyone who knows me, they will say I am not easily stopped. As a Busy mum of four children, with multiple businesses, and jobs on the go, I am always running. Always busy, juggling work, juggling children's activities, as well as various therapies, like Speech, physio and OT. I have always thrived on being busy. I don't like sitting still, I never have.

I have always been like that, I can't sit still, can't stop. Even when pregnant, I didn't let anything slow me down. I worked up until two days before my first was born whilst suffering hyperemesis gravidarum (HG), vomiting 30 plus times a day, and then decided to go back and do it again, three more times. Ten days after my daughter was born, whilst still nursing a third-degree tear, we decided to drive from Melbourne to Batemans Bay, to deliver a forgotten caravan door. So slowing down, or stopping is not something I do.

But in April 2020 at the beginning of the Covid-19 Pandemic, I came down with the flu, and I was knocked for six. I didn't get of the couch for a couple of days. For the first time in a very long time, I had no choice, I had to stop.

I had recently flown back from visiting my Dad who was in hospital in Melbourne, the hospital he had been at had been one of the first testing hospitals for COVID, so when I began to get symptoms of the flu, of course, my mind rushed to the pandemic that was starting to spread around the World.

As the fear about COVID was growing, and my breathing became labored, I headed down to our local emergency department, not realizing this visit would be a glimpse into the new normal we'd all soon be living in. At the time I found it amusing, not realizing how much of an effect COVID would have on interactions we would have in a medical setting in the future.

As I walked up to the emergency department, the nurse apologetically told me I couldn't come in, as I had cold and flu symptoms. I would need to head next door and get tested for Covid first, and then follow their new guidelines.

I wandered back outside struggling to breathe, and headed next door to the Testing facility. Now this was at the start of covid when you had to be assessed first as to whether your symptoms were severe enough for a test, so even though they wouldn't let me enter the emergency department there was no guarantee they would also test me for COVID.

So I headed next door to the testing area, where I talked to someone over the phone, and explained my symptoms, coupled with my recent flights to Melbourne, they decided that I should be tested. I sat there whilst the nurse pocked the foot-long probe into my nose and throat, pushing it so far back you felt like she was going to damage something, and then they said to head next door to be assessed by the emergency department.

As I walked towards the emergency department struggling to breathe, the nurse looked at me through his PPE, and I imagine he smiled at me, but I couldn't tell through the heavy mask and plastic cover. He pointed towards the park bench near the entrance, So there I was back sitting outside on the park bench, waiting to be triaged.

Ten minutes later, the nurse came over decked out in full PPE from head to toe. He reassured me and began to triage me outside the entrance of the Emergency department on a park bench, he kept apologizing that I couldn't go inside the hospital, I could hear the compassion in his voice. So there I sat, whilst the nurse checked my blood pressure, and filled out the forms, outside on a cold park bench. Once he had finished triaging me, I remember sending my husband a message, half in disbelief, saying, "I never thought I'd see the day where I'd be triaged outside the front of a hospital in Australia."

So there I sat outside on the park bench for over an hour and a half, waiting for someone to leave the COVID-19 ward so I could be admitted, I watched as the other park benches began filling up, with other patients waiting, feeling too sick to leave, but feeling worse every minute I sat outside in the elements, thankful that I was on the Sunshine Coast and not stuck outside a Melbourne hospital in the colder weather.

Even then when I was admitted, everything was so different. The hospitals were still trying to work out how best to combat COVID, so I sat behind a glass door in the makeshift COVID ward, alone.

I think they had converted a children's ward into a COVID ward as colorful pictures lined the walls, obviously aimed at children. A nurse in full PPE came in attached leads for an ECG, took my blood, re-did my blood pressure, and handed me an x-ray film, she explained that they would have to take an X-ray of my chest through the glass window as they did not want to risk any contamination on the machine.

All communication was done over the phone, with nurses, and doctors watching through the glass. At one point, The doctor casually mentioned in passing, oh it looks like your heart skipped a beat whilst we were doing the

ECG, but didn't seem worried, they let me know the chest x-ray was clear, my oxygen level was a little low but nothing to worry about. They told me to head home, drink fluids, and have Panadol, to make sure I rest and wait for my results. Everyone in the family had to quarantine until we got my results. No one mentioned that I should get the heart issue checked, there was nothing noted in my file or on my discharge paperwork.

I waited and two days later on 2nd April, I got the news I was hoping for, it wasn't COVID, just the normal flu, Little did I know that eight months later I would be back in a different hospital dealing with the ramifications of that flu.

Wife, Mother, Twin.

If you were asked to say three words to describe you, what would they be?

Some people use descriptive words to describe what they look like, how they feel, but I know that can change, for me three simple words come to mind.

Wife, Mother, Twin!

I was born in 1982, 5 days after my older sister's second birthday. At the time, my parents were living on a remote farm in Tasmania, but when they found out they were expecting twins, they moved back to Victoria for our birth. My sister and I were born at Sandringham Hospital in Melbourne. I was born first by thirteen minutes.

Three years later our youngest sister came along, and just under two years later, my brother would be born, making our family complete. The five of us siblings, all with very distinct personalities, but bound together by shared experiences and a unique upbringing.

If I had to sum up my childhood in one word, it would be colorful. My dad was best described as a free spirit, he was a hippy, not one to follow the rules of society, this is highlighted when a few years ago when I was organizing my children's passports I happened to take a look at my birth certificate. I scanned down and when I got to the job description of my father, it read 'Lead Light artist'. I don't know why I found it so amusing but it just seemed to capture him so perfectly, creative, unconventional, and always a bit outside the box.

Whilst he was a Plumber by trade, most of his working life was spent in the rock and roll industry, wheeling and dealing or things adjacent to that. He was the life of the party a very big personality, and growing up within that environment is not one I would want for my children, but as a child, it is the life you know.

He never wanted to settle down, and our childhood involved a lot of new schools, new friends, new houses, never staying for more than a couple of years in one place, our schooling and home life were all over the place, and change was the only constant.

Stability was never high on my dad's priority list.

He struggled to hold a job, self-employment suited him better, as he had to be the boss, had to be in charge, and had to follow his own rules. His temper, his frustration, and his inability to fit the mold of employment meant that most of the time he went into 'normal' employment it didn't last long. In the house, it was the same. The house followed his rules, and you didn't dare push back, as you wouldn't want to deal with the consequences.

My Dad was a storyteller, and he would charm everyone who met him, he was the life of the party, and he always seemed to know the important people. He thrived in social situations. He was confident, he seemed to get energy from being around people, he was eccentric, a lot of fun, but that fun came at a cost. A cost that at times his family had to pay.

But through it all, was my mother, She was the stability in our family, she worked tirelessly as a nurse, night shift. She was maternal, she was gracious, she was loving, and she was enough.

My twin sister and I, are very close, we shared a room up until I got married and moved out, and to this day we talk every day. My husband thankfully understands this closeness, and still finds it amusing, that when she lived around the corner we would often spend the day together, and then before we had even got home, we'd already be on the phone again.

We spent years being called Twin 1 and Twin 2, and for some time tried to pretend we weren't twins, we would catch the bus home sitting in separate seats, but the minute we would get off the bus we would start talking. Considering we looked alike, I don't know what we were trying to prove. I think part of the problem was that being a teenager is hard, you are already trying to find out who you are, and when you are a twin that becomes even harder. People without meaning to, always compare you, and when the person they are comparing you to, is going through the same stages at the same time. The pressure can become unbearable.

We had friends that didn't help as they refused to hang out with us on their own as in their mind it looked like they didn't have many friends if they hung out with two near identical sisters. Thankfully this stage and these friends didn't last that long. We not only found friends who didn't care that were twins, but we also decided that we did enjoy each other's company.

We played sports together, I was and still is, the competitive one, My sister was the friendly one who would make friends with the opposition, spending her time apologizing if my competitive streak became a bit too much. I have to admit it did at times, we always played mixed sports, and It didn't matter to me whether I was coming up against guys twice my size, my objective was the same, to get that ball. I wish there were the same opportunities back then for women's sports as there are now.

We both got jobs together at Safeway, initially separating us into separate departments to spare confusion. I have to admit I felt like I got the short straw, as a vegetarian I was offered a job working in the deli, and Bek became a check-out operator.

Our interests were very similar, we both took up singing, and each week we would head to the footy with our Nana, cheering on the Saints, our weekends would be spent walking down the beach, talking, and just enjoying each other's company. We were the best of friends, something we still are years later.

My fondest memories are the early years of school before the schools separated us. In the early years, we had our own language twin talk (Cryptophasia), this is something I wish we had more records of, but our childhood was before the age of iPhones, and videos. I remember a few words, pencil was Mensa, and our sister was goo-gee, but the words are all lost to time now, and we would often be lost in our own conversations.

Once we hit Grade 2, the school decided it would be in our best interest to separate us, but as soon as the bell would ring we would find each other. Our friends a mix from each of our classes, well except for those two years in early high school when we pretended we weren't twins. When we bought our friend's home, all of a sudden we would all become good friends. Even now we still have a large group of friends from school, and are still affectionately called the "twins".

Our personalities have always complemented each other, Bek is very clean and organized, if she is having a bad day she loves to clean and reorganize cupboards, whereas I would retreat into my imagination, escape in my notebook my computer to write poems and stories. Our bedroom was the cliche twin room, split in two, her side neat and organized, my side a chaotic mess of Stkilda football club newspaper clippings, and an 'organized mess'.

Our childhood was very different to most, our Dad had a savior complex and we grew up with Alcoholics and drug addicts in our house Dad was trying to help overcome their addictions, so we retreated to our room, finding refuge in each other and our imagination.

Our friendship is forged in memories and stories, some memories we cherish, others we would love to forget. I would say our childhood has offered us a shared resilience. A resilience that has helped us both through the challenges we faced as adults.

I have two best friends in life, my husband and my twin sister. Maybe that has been to my detriment as even now twenty odd years after I have finished school, I have found it hard to make friends If I am having a bad day I call my husband or my sister, I have never had to or even tried to rely on anyone else. But I wouldn't change things as they both understand me and who I am, and I cherish them both.

I grew up going to church and my faith is a big part of who I am, I don't believe I would have got through what I have had to face without my faith grounding me.

I met my husband about three or four years before we got together, I was babysitting for some friends, their young daughter was asleep and I had sat down to watch a corny chick flick. It's funny the memories that stick in your mind. I can still remember the movie. Emma starring Gwyneth Paltrow, an adaptation of the Jane Austen novel.

I had just put the kids to bed, and I heard a knock at the door. Startled I answered it to find three or four young guys at the door. My friends had neglected to tell me that his younger brother and his mates would be heading down to go surfing the next day.

My face was red, something that happened to me frequently at that age, I had to deal with the pure embarrassment of sitting through the last half of a corny Jane Austen movie with four guys commentary. If I had realized they were coming I would have chosen a very different movie. Some random action movie with very little storyline.

It was some years later that he moved to the Peninsula where I lived, and our friendship grew, just before my nineteenth birthday, those friends became my brother and sister-in-law. Some people would say I married early and in today's time I guess I did, but many years later I still know it was the best decision I have ever made.

Together we have had four beautiful children, and have run successful businesses together, we have traveled Australia, and the world, so I am happy to describe myself as ***Wife, Mother, Twin***.

My Life.

Our married life began in Langwarrin a place I still look at fondly, Though we married early we weren't in a hurry to have a family. We wanted time to establish ourselves financially, time to travel and to explore more of Australia. We valued the idea of building a strong relationship first, before growing our family.

The interesting thing is, the passion to travel, to explore, to build financial freedom didn't change after our children were born. Having children didn't stop us from pursuing our dreams or from seeing Australia and the world, it just makes the journey even more exciting. We continued to travel, but now, it was with our children in tow. So many people tell you to travel whilst you are young, and whilst that is true, travelling and living your life should happen at any stage.

When we were pregnant with our first Child, a very wise mum said to us. "When you have children they should fit into your life, They add to it. Make sure that they fit in with your routine, not the other way around. We realised we loved travelling, loved going to the beach, listening to music. So very quickly we made sure our children, were a part of our lives, part of the things that mattered to us.

Our children have been very fortunate to have traveled extensively, both within Australia and beyond. Our oldest two have visited some simply breathtaking places like Athabasca Falls, they have crossed the vast Nullarbor multiple times, they have walked through canyons in the Northern Territory, and even ventured to the very tip of Australia, Cape York. They have set foot in every state and territory in Australia, gaining a very deep appreciation for Australia's rich culture and heritage.

Our younger two have also traveled extensively in Australia, and hopefully, soon they will be able to make it to Western Australia, so they can say they have been to every state and territory in Australia. They too have experienced incredible adventures. with us and their older siblings they have road-tripped through America, exploring the highways and hidden treasures of the States, they have visited the happiest place on earth, have cruised to the Bahamas, and even traveled through Thailand, soaking in the rich culture and landscapes.

I look back at my childhood where I can count on my hand the holidays I had, and feel that I have given my child a real sense of wanderlust and desire to travel.

Looking back to the years after our daughter was born, my husband spent some time helping his mum prepare her business for sale, her business sale settled a few weeks before my twin sister's wedding in Queensland, and this allowed us to take a six week trip through Queensland in a Jayco Eagle. I was over six months pregnant at the time, and during that trip, as we sat in a caravan park on the Sunshine Coast, we decided that Scott would take a job he had been offered on the Gold Coast.

When we make a decision, we run with it, and only a few weeks later we packed up our life in the back of a Hertz rental van, and we were on the way. Whilst we enjoyed the weather, after six months with a 2 year old and a 5 month old in tow, we decided to move back to Victoria back closer to family. The 2000kms were just to far with two young children. We wanted them to grow up knowing their Aunties and Uncles. Family was too important to us, to be so far away.

Though we often wish we had stayed in Queensland and instead had taken the time to talk Bek and her husband into moving to us, without the move back to Melbourne, we wouldn't have bought our business and moved to Ballarat, which is a huge part of our story. I am a firm believer in no regrets.

You can't regret the path you have taken, it's all part of the adventure.

We loved Ballarat, it was home, we had a business there, we had a life, beautiful memories with our children, and it is somewhere I still look at fondly, There is such rich history in Ballarat, everybody talks about Sovereign hill, but it is more than that. The grand wide streets, lined with old heritage listed buildings, relics of the Gold rush Era, mixed in with new more modern buildings, give the city a unique charm.

The town whilst only over an hour from Melbourne still has a country town feel, I remember a few years in my Nana had a heart attack and I called the school to let them know I would have to pick up the kids early, and when I arrived they handed me a precooked Lasagne so I didn't have to worry about cooking that night. It was such a simple act, but one that surprised me growing up in the City.

Some people ask us how long we stayed in Ballarat, and we always tell them we spent twelve cold winters in Ballarat. People laugh, but if you have ever spent any time there in winter you understand. There is something about the feeling of cold in Ballarat. It wasn't just a temperature but it was an atmosphere. In Ballarat everyone has a uniform, a Kathmandu jacket, I think everyone lasts about half a year, before they succumb and venture down to Mair Street and come home with their own.

But the cold weather was something that we never quite adjusted to, our heater was always set to Queensland temperature, and we would flee the cold weather for 6 – 8 weeks each year to Queensland trying to defrost. At first, we thought Ballarat might be the place that we settled in for good. We loved its history, the community, the pace of life. But something about the cold always lingered, reminding us that perhaps our true home would eventually lead us back to the warmth of Queensland.

Every time we would holiday in Queensland, I would jokingly say, we should move back, however, our life and work kept us in Ballarat, but one day I said it, in front of our kids, and the two older two, said Yes, let's do it. I knew that I could never retire in Ballarat, as great as it was, I craved the beach, the warmth, and the thought of moving away from my kids, when they got older is also something I couldn't do, So we decided we needed to find a way to make it work to make the move early enough when our children would come with us and hopefully become settled in Queensland and create their own lives there as well.

In 2019, just a few months before COVID-19 would start to turn the world upside down, we made the move. We packed all our stuff in a U-haul trailer and began the drive to our new home. After our previous time on the Gold Coast, we decided we wanted something a bit quieter, a bit more like the country lifestyle our children were used to, so we decided to head further up the coast of Queensland towards the Sunshine Coast, away from the hustle and bustle of the Gold Coast. Sunshine Coast has the community spirit that we had come to love from Ballarat, but with Queensland temperature.

It felt like the right decision, and I truly believe it was life-changing for me, as I always wondered if I didn't move to Queensland and decide to make the choices that I did, the choice to join Crossfit, and attempt to get fit, begin tracking my sleep, and go to a GP that took my concerns seriously, would I still be here to enjoy the life that I am so grateful to have.

August 2020

After our move to Queensland, we initially kept our business in Victoria, renting a little old miners cottage a short walk from Sovereign Hill. At first, managing it from Queensland wasn't too difficult, whilst my husband didn't like traveling for work, he only had to travel down once a fortnight, a quick flight, a two-night stay, and then he was home again. But when COVID hit everything started to get so much harder. Flights became scarce, unpredictable, and incredibly expensive.

He was still needed down south, our business, and our thirty staff relied on him. So he started driving down, a 2000km journey each way, it wasn't ideal but unfortunately it was necessary. Due to the length of the drive, he would stay longer, at least a week at a time to make the long drive worth it. Whilst others might not mind FIFO life, it was not something we had ever imagined for ourselves.

We are that couple that goes to bed at the same time each night, and without a lot of family support have always relied on each other, so it took its toll on us. The day before he had to leave we would all feel it, the mood would shift considerably in the house. No one wanted to focus on the sad goodbye again the next day.

The strain of balancing the business with our family life in Queensland was growing, Running a retail business in the middle of a global pandemic was pressure enough, but then navigating the home/work balance with no family support in Queensland continued to add to the stress, so it was a real relief when someone approached us to buy the business, we knew that it was time to seriously consider the offer.

I remember walking down Main Beach feeling the water on my feet, as we sat and talked over the offer. The idea of finishing the chapter of our lives felt right, a chance to get ourselves settled in Queensland, without the constant pull back to Victoria.

Trying to sell a business in another state in the middle of COVID-19 was not ideal, and there were logistical challenges at every turn. Around the time of settlement, the government imposed stricter quarantine measures, and started imposing strict border closures and implementing mandatory hotel quarantine. So the costs began to stack up as we had to arrange to transport both our cars back up from Victoria and fly back to Queensland after the sale.

Returning to Queensland also meant that we had to spend two weeks in Hotel quarantine, with our four kids. As an adult full of responsibilities at first there was something nice about sitting in a hotel room, with food being given to you three times a day. No cleaning, no dishes, but after a day or two, you begin to crave the freedom, you realise that there is only so much TV you can watch especially with an eight year old who wants to sit between her mum and Dad as she craved social interaction.

We watched that many home renovation and other lifestyle shows, it took me another 6 months to watch another one after we got out.

After a few days the food whilst nutritionally sound, started to begin tasting the same. You had no choice you just received a meal and hoped it was something you liked, the selection wasn't great for children, so we were thankful that we could still order Uber eats, and had a large amount of 2 minute noodles to heat up. We did learn very quickly though that we could only choose food from Uber eats that it didn't matter if it sat at reception for a long time, as there was strict rules on who could deliver the food to our room, and often you would wait 20-30 minutes for someone to be able to bring it upstairs. The kids would excitedly wait for the knock at the door, then stand waiting long enough so the person had enough time to drop the food and be metres away before they answered the door.

We attempted to go downstairs for the daily exercise time, but our children found it very confronting, we were allowed to walk around the large concrete area, but had to be more than 3m from anyone else. The yard guarded by police and military personal making sure no one went to close to each other, or tried to escape. Up until that time it didn't feel real to our children a great excuse to watch movies and play on devices, but the exercise time really upset them all and bought it back home that they couldn't leave the hotel, so instead we decided to forgo the exercise time and instead try and exercise in our hotel room.

We were lucky and had two interconnecting rooms that had a connected balcony, so we would have to kids walk out our balcony door, and in the adjoining room via the balcony and do laps of the room for ten to fifteen minutes a couple of times a day, just to get them up and moving.

Whilst it was a challenge we all knew it was worth it to start our life afresh in Queensland, knowing our focus now could be on our future.

After the stress of running our own business, and with COVID-19 still affecting the economy and businesses everywhere, we made a conscious decision to take some time off, to get fit, and prioritise spend some time with the kids before we stepped into another business and all the stresses associated with it.

After years of hard work, and cold Victorian weather we joined a local CrossFit gym, and decided it was time to start to get fit. The previous few years had been quite rough on my body, with a failed uterine ablation followed by a Hysterectomy due to Adenomyosis and severe iron deficiency so my starting fitness was almost non-existent. But each day bought a little bit of progress, it was less about loosing weight, and more about creating a new routine, a new normal.

Our days became a nice routine, most mornings we would go to a CrossFit class, followed by a walk, and pick up the kids from school. My fitness started improving, little by little and I felt the best I had in years. It's amazing the difference having correct iron levels, and regular exercise has to your overall well-being.

As the months went by and my fitness improved, I decided to track my sleep once again on my Apple Watch, something I had been doing in the past. That's when I started noticing that I had received notifications overnight about a low heart rate. I brushed it off, thinking it was nothing serious.

One morning my phone beeped again, 'Low heart rate' This time though I was too slow to dismiss it, and My husband looked at the alert. The concern etched into his face, I downplayed it, not telling him it had been coming up for nearly 5 months now. He told me to get it checked out. I reasoned my mum and my sister have naturally low resting heart rates, and I just put it down to a family trait, my twin sister had even spent money on a cardiologist just to be told it was perfectly normal. I was heading off on a trip to visit Mum soon, I felt so much better than I had in years so what was the point?

Scott, however, was slowly noticing something I couldn't. Instead of continuing to improve at CrossFit, I was getting increasingly fatigued after each CrossFit class. Still, as I always do, I pushed through. I was exercising, I was losing weight, I was loving our life in Queensland. Why should a minor alert on my watch cause me to worry when everything else felt so good?

But that small notification would soon become impossible to ignore.

November 13th – 16th 2020

Sitting here looking over all my notes, I hate to admit how long I ignored the Low heart rate notifications before I did something about it. When I went back and looked at my health app on my phone, I was startled to realise that the first alert was on the 10th April 2020, just over a week after my visit to the hospital. But back then, I brushed it off, life was busy that I ignored it, I made excuses, I didn't have the time to be sick, we had a business sale to worry about, I didn't have the time to deal with it. I hide the alerts from everyone as I didn't want anyone unnecessarily worrying about me. I convinced myself it wasn't important.

But that all changed when I flew up to visit my mum in Cairns at the end of Spring, in November of 2020, 7 months after the first alert.

On the first morning of my quick weekend with my mum, I sat at her dining room table, looking out the window at the lush tropical landscape of her apartment in Cairns, the heat and humidity were already starting to settle in for the day, and I could faintly hear the water in the background, the birds sing, its peaceful and relaxing. We sit in silence, enjoying the stillness of the morning. Very different to my normal busy mornings back home. We had just gone for a long walk along the beach, before the heat of the day. We sat in comfortable silence, mum with her cuppa, me with my cold glass of water.

An audible alert on my watch, cut through the silence. I stop and stare at my watch and my mum's eyes instinctively follow. Low heart rate notification 33 beats per minute. I tried to dismiss it quickly, however I wasn't quick enough.

Mum has a puzzled look on her face, "What's that?" her tone laced with concern.
"Oh Nothing", I attempt to laugh it off. "My watch just thinks my heart rate is low sometimes."
"How low?" she pressed.

I look down at the watch, "33 beats per minute" even I have to admit that is the lowest I have seen it beep at me. "Don't worry mum" I add quickly "you know your heart rate is low, and so is Bek's, it's probably just a genetic thing, my watch sometimes tells me my heart rate is low, but it's nothing to worry about.",

I notice the concern in her eyes, "Sarah, ours is low, but not that low, You need to go see someone, just to get it checked."

"I will talk to some one next time I go to the Doctor, its nothing to worry about mum" I tried once again to downplay it, saying all the excuses I had been saying to myself for months. "We have been walking all morning, do I look like someone who is sick?"

She smiled skeptically, "I know you, you will get busy and put it off again, how long has this been happening for?"

"A little while" I reply, trying to think of how long the alerts had been happening for.

"Why don't you just book online, I am sure your doctor would take online bookings wouldn't they?"

Reluctantly I reach for me phone, and decided to book an appointment not because I was worried, but more just to get it over and done with. Also because I knew that now between Mum and my husband who had also recently found out about the alerts, they would keep pestering me until I did something. I don't expect anything to be wrong. I had just walked 5 km that morning with Mum through the humidity and I felt fine. I felt like booking a doctors appointment would be a huge waste of my time.

But maybe it was as I was relaxed, enjoying the serenity, but as I sat at Mum's kitchen table, I pick up my iPhone and log into my doctor's online booking system to book an appointment, My doctor is notoriously hard to get into, the first available appointment wasn't until the 10th of December, nearly a month later, so I book it, and then go back to enjoying my weekend away, pushing the whole thing out of my mind.

That was until I was awoken suddenly at 1:51 am, by another notification on my phone "Low heart rate detected". The frequency of the alerts was growing, and although I kept dismissing them, a small part of me couldn't shake the feeling, that maybe something wasn't right.

10th December 2020

I wander into my GP's office, feeling a little ridiculous that I am bringing up a warning from a watch. I feel fine, great even, I have been exercising consistently, 4-5 days a week, building up my strength, and endurance. I had just gone for a run the other day, the first run I had done, since my fourth child was born. Compared to my past I am so much healthier, and fitter, and I have started to lose weight. For the first time in a long time, I felt great. Honestly, I wasn't at all concerned. We had just bought a house and had just started busy packing all our stuff up for our new house. We had decided it was time to start looking for a new business venture. Life was good.

I wander in by myself, Scott at home with the four kids. I wasn't worried at all, I was even slightly embarrassed bringing up the notification. The appointment was casual, My GP went through all my history and checked my Blood pressure, it's low, but that's not out of the ordinary for me, I have always had low to normal BP. He smiles, as I explain why I am here. It seems like he is not too worried as well. His reassuring voice and relaxed tone, "It's probably not something to worry about you could just be fit". I smile politely, but in my mind, I'm thinking, ***Fit? After just six months of***

working out? I'm not sure about that. While I've been sticking to a consistent fitness routine, I wouldn't say I've reached athlete-level conditioning.

My GP, though, remains relaxed and unhurried, which eases any lingering concern I might have had. But, just to be on the safe side, he suggests we do an ECG—"just in case," he says. It's nothing urgent, and they can do it right there in the office, so I agree. So 5 minutes later I was wandering back into his room, to get my result, I fully expected to hear "All Clear".

As he looked over my ECG, his brow furrowed slightly, and I remember him saying something like. "Oh, that's a bit strange you have an irregular heartbeat. He explains that it's not always something to worry about but he would feel better if I saw a cardiologist just in case." I remember back to the hospital visit 8 months early and the comment about my heart skipping a beat, I think to myself *The doctor at the hospital wasn't worried, maybe it's related to that.*

I am what people call an eternal optimist, you don't support a team like St'Kilda Football Club through the 90s and beyond and not be one. So even after hearing him call the cardiologist office to squeeze me in, I continued to brush it off, still not concerned, But maybe that should have been a clue, as he didn't just send the referral letter, he called the office directly and organised the appointment with the Cardiologist, only four weeks later just after Christmas. I realize now how lucky I was to get in that quickly. Most people without a history of heart attacks are waiting three months or more to see a cardiologist. At the time, though, I didn't give it a second thought.

When I got home, I casually tell Scott. "It's really nothing to worry about," I assure him. "They just want to me to see a Cardiologist to double-check the results, but I'm sure everything's fine." We had enough on our plate to worry about with the upcoming move, finishing the school year, the cardiologist was just another appointment on my calendar, something to check off.

We had a fantastic holiday season, visits down to the Gold Coast, riding rollercoaster under sparkling lights at night at Movie world for their Christmas event, mornings relaxing at the beach and by the pool, just spending time celebrating with our kids. The thoughts of low heart rates, cardiologist faded into the background as we focused on the holiday season and packing and cleaning the house for our upcoming move.

But the appointment was there on the Calendar inching closer, looking back, I am so grateful that we didn't know what we were about to face. Our days were filled without any worry or uncertainty just hope. We had that month to live in the present, no work, no school, a new house, a new dream. We were preparing for a fresh start. We went to bed each night, exhausted but happy.

For a moment, each night before my watch would remind me with an alert, life was as I felt it should be, busy, hopeful and filled with joy.

12th January 2021

I wander into my cardiologist appointment, glancing around the waiting room, its very quiet, I smile at the other half a dozen patients waiting. It's very different to the normal waiting rooms I go to, instead of the hustle and bustle with young families around. Here I was at least half the age of all the other patients waiting, and I thought to myself. *Do I really need to be here?*. I am mentally preparing for a stress test to show that I am not as fit as I hope, a quick reassuring conversation, and a large bill and nothing more.

I sit smiling watching the people's name be called one by one, concern etched on the faces of the person they are sitting with. I notice I am the only one who came alone. But I couldn't imagine my four kids in the waiting room. When the cardiologist finally calls my name, his manner is calm, professional but still reassuring, "Look, it's probably not a problem", he said. "Most times people will have an irregular heartbeat but it won't be a problem. However, let's run some tests just in case. His words are comforting, and I'm still feeling confident that I'll be in and out, with nothing major to worry about.

I met my nurse we did an ultrasound on my heart, An echocardiogram (The first of many I will have) and we did a Stress test, I don't seem to be long into my stress test, and my doctor stopped it quite suddenly. I was surprised, I was expecting it to be arduous, I didn't feel like I had reached any kind of limit, I wasn't any more out of breath than normal. I look at him, almost expecting an explanation for cutting it short, however instead his expression slightly changes, I can see a seriousness in his face I hadn't seen before.

He tells me to get dressed, and grab the person I came with, and head into his office. My heart begins to beat a bit faster. Instinctively I knew at that moment it wasn't good news, this was not routine anymore. I go quiet, I am by myself, I didn't bring anyone with me.

When he notices I am alone, He pauses, and his demeanour changes, "No, you shouldn't be by yourself, is someone picking you up?" I smile politely and tell him no, I left my husband at home with our four kids, 40 minutes away, moving into our new house. I mentioned that we're in Queensland with no family nearby, so no, there's no one waiting for me. It's just me. He nods but his expression doesn't change.

He looks at me, "No you shouldn't be alone" almost like him telling me again could make someone magically appear to stay with me. I smile again awkwardly, as I follow him towards his room, I respond quietly, "But I am alone". I feel like that scene in Clueless when Cher walks down the street with *All by myself* playing softly in the background.

I wander behind him into his office, its a large room, staring across from him, the seat beside me empty, a glaring reminder that I was in fact, by myself. He took a deep breathe, my heart begins to beat even louder in my chest. Then he delivers the news I wasn't expecting to hear. "Unfortunately, in your case," he began gently, "I know I talked to you about how sometimes irregular heart beats are not a big problem, in your case the irregular heartbeat is a big problem, it is not something we can ignore. We need to run more tests to be sure of what's going on, but there is obvious damage to your heart, we'll have a better picture once we get the results from a 24-hour heart monitor, then we can see how many of your beats are irregular. When you come back to discuss the results," he pauses and stared at me with an intense gaze, "you shouldn't come alone."

The weight of his words sinks in slowly, but I'm still not fully grasping the gravity of the situation. I nod, and mutter a quick Thanks. I head to reception to pick up the heart monitor, going through the motions, feeling a bit detached from the reality that something is wrong with my heart. I know I have to call Scott and let him know he is expecting a phone call, but neither of us, where expecting the call to be like this. *Damage to my heart*. What did that mean.

I dial Scott on the way out, but the phone

drops out almost instantly, the coverage in the underground carpark is spotty at times, as I drive off it still feels surreal, we got the keys to our new house yesterday, and now I will be all hooked up to a heart monitor whilst I help move into the house. This was not the plan.

I get through and relay the information to Scott, but keep it casual, not focusing on the part about damage to my heart, I focus more on they need to run more tests and I am hooked up to a heart monitor, so warn the kids that mum has cords attached.

I'd spent my whole life trusting that my heart was there, steady and reliable, just doing it job in the background. Now, for the first time, that sense of security felt shaken. I hadn't fully accepted it yet, what it meant, or what it would mean for my future, my families future.

I still hadn't fully accepted that my heart, something that's always just worked might not be as dependable as I thought.

Moving Home

13th January 2021

The Queensland heat in January can be unforgiving, wrapping itself around you, making even the smallest task seem exhausting. Moving into our new house should have been an exciting milestone, but as we moved boxes around, rearranging furniture, I was painfully aware of the wires and monitor criss crossing across my chest. It was hard to ignore them.

I tried to allow the busyness and the chaos of the day to help me escape the thoughts that tried to invade my mind. But every time my perspiration would cause the adhesive to come loose, the machine would beep and I would have to stop what I was doing a reattach the wire, and I would be bought back to reality. How was I here, only two days ago, life was normal, busy but manageable, however now something was wrong with my heart, the invisible driving force of my body.

This is not what I was expecting when we purchased our new home two months earlier, I wasn't expecting to be hooked up to multitude of cords, and a heart monitor, meeting our new neighbours. I expected to be swimming in our new pool with the kids, moving boxes, celebrating our new house. Instead, here I was, awkwardly greeting our new neighbours, on our new driveway, my eyes darting around to make sure my the wires weren't to obvious as they peeked out from under my shirt as we had a casual conversation.

I couldn't help but feel self-conscious as I smiled, and shook hands, wishing I was wearing a different shirt that hid the monitor better.

As if right on cue, in the middle of a conversation, my watch pinged with yet another low-heart notification. I feel the faint vibration on my wrist and look down, hoping the neighbours don't notice the distraction. At first, the low heart rate notifications only happened overnight, but now they happen at any time of the day interrupting conversations. They now held a heavier weight than they did even two days earlier, they were now a reminder that something was wrong.

I smiled and nodded, pretending everything was fine, but was reminded of my heart's unpredictability. I tried to brush it off as I had done for the last eight months, but the parting comment from the cardiologist the day before had made it hard.

"When you come back, don't come alone!"

Its funny that the words 'you heart is damaged, didn't hold the same weight as "Don't come alone" those words had anchored deep in my mind, chipping away at my optimism. The thought shook me, I couldn't protect Scott if he was sitting beside me, I couldn't downplay anything, I couldn't brush it away, reframe it. I would have to deal with it.

For the first time in a long time, I was vulnerable, I had spent so many of my years, protecting myself from that feeling, I had learnt to downplay things, to focus on the positive, to be the strong one. I was an optimist it was as much as my identity as being a mother, a wife and a twin. But this was something I couldn't brush off, explain away, or put off any longer. In a few weeks when he finished going through all the data, there would be no hiding anymore.

I couldn't protect Scott or myself from Bad news, If he was there sitting beside me in the doctors office, he would hear everything. The thought of allowing someone else to help me, to be vulnerable was not a feeling I ever wanted to be. I was strong, I was optimistic, I was a survivor. I always felt like it was my job as a mother, as a carer to be the one to carry others, to hold it together, to be strong. It was a role I took on at a very early age through the ups and downs of our childhood. I didn't want to be the one who needed reassurance, I didn't want to be the one who needed help, truthfully I didn't know if I could even sit in that role.

I was defenceless, in a few weeks, we would be sitting in the cardiologist office and whatever news the doctor would give us, we would have to face it together. Only time would tell if I would let my guard down and let Scott hold the burden for me, for now all I could do was pray that the results were better than the doctors parting words had suggested.

The Question of Resilence.

As I look back at my journey, I think I can say that I am resilient. But where does that come from? Is resilience something that you are born with, a trait tucked hidden within our DNA, our personality, or is it something that life carves into you, piece by piece, through all the different experiences we face.

Its the age old debate.

Nature vs Nurture.

Did that colourful, sometimes tumultuous childhood I talked about previously, full of insecurity, moving schools, having to make new friends, leaving old ones, help build the traits I would need for this journey, lay the foundation for the resilence I would need for the journey ahead. Was it the faith that I have, that helped build the optimism that would be needed to get up each day, knowing that no matter what there is something to hope for, something to hope in, something to hold onto?

Is it the small setbacks, the daily ups and downs, that help prepare us for the bigger moments? Or is the life altering moments, the ones that shake us to the core, that truly build our strength?

I remember vividly, as a child one of those moments, we were in early high school, and for some reason, I had stayed behind at school, perhaps for sport, or choir, the reason is long lost to history know, whilst Bek, my twin, had headed home on the bus by herself.

I arrived home and the house was empty, As I went to the kitchen to grab something to eat, and I heard the phone ring, it was the hospital, Bek had been struck by a car at speed, on her way home from school.

Bek had been crossing a busy highway at a designated crossing area, not a pedestrian one, but one where there is a curb set out so you know thats where you need to cross, and someone had come around the corner a little two fast, not paying attention, and she was hit, she had bounced over the car and then landed roughly on the highway behind.

But someone was looking after her that day, and as luck would have it, the next car to come around the corner was a paramedic. Who rushed out and offered quick care. They waited with her until another ambulance arrived to take her to the hospital. This was before smart watches, and even before we had mobile phones, so when Bek got to the hospital, they tried home, and got no-one, but she called a friends parent who came in with her and waited, until they could reach my mum.

Bek was ok, given the circumstances, however half of her face and part of one side of her body had been badly damaged by the road as she had scrapped along it, after hitting the car and being propelled over it and onto the road. As I watched her recover from it, not just the physical scars, but the emotional ones, it was hard, as a twin, our bond was different, and it had always been my role, to try and protect her, just as she protected me, we protected each other, but in this case, this was her story, this was her recovery, this was her pain. I couldn't shield her from the pain, or help speed up any healing. For the first time, I felt truly powerless. Was that what helped build my resilience for times in the future when I would feel powerless, overwhelmed.

As twins, it's funny how so many of our stories begin with *we* instead of *I*. It's almost instinctive. For as long as I can remember, life has been experienced through the lens of *us*. From the moment we were born, our identities were intertwined. It wasn't just *me* going to school for the first time—it was *us*. It wasn't just *me* learning to navigate friendships, struggles, and triumphs—it was *us*.

But this was a journey that was hers, and watching her, being inspired by her, Is that what helped grow my resilience?

When Bek was hit by a car, I wasn't there in the moment, but it still felt like it happened to us, I remember the sick feeling in my stomach, when it happened the feeling of utter helplessness with the phone call, my best friend, someone who is as much a part of my story as me, was hurt, and I was powerless to help.

Being a twin doesn't mean you are the same person, however we have a shared history, a shared story, that is impossible to seperate. Every story, every memory is filtered through the connection we share. Maybe thats why my resilience doesn't feel like something I learned on my own, it feels like a shared lesson, from every set back, both individually, and together.

It's not to say our journey's aren't also singular, we both have our own unique path, unique stories, especially as we have both grown up, got married, had our own children, had our own setbacks, however there is and will always be a sense of we, a shared strength, shared stories, shared laughter, and even shared tears. That has always been there, quietly shaping how I see the world.

Looking at things from that lens, really helps you look at the Nature vs nurture. Maybe resilience is a bit of both, it's an inherent part of who we are, and part of who we become through life's ups and downs, through every trial, and every triumph.

What I know for sure is that resilience doesn't mean never falling, in life it's impossible to never fall down. But It means standing back up again and again, hopefully stronger, wiser each time, ready for whatever comes next.

The World Turned Upside Down

8th February 2021

So back to the day that my world turned upside down. As we walked out of the appointment, our minds were reeling, struggling to process everything. My legs felt heavy as we wandered slowly past the room, once again filled with elderly patients, it struck me how out of place I felt, I was only in my 30s and surrounded by people over twice my age. It was jarring to realize that I too, now belonged in this room, this room of heart patients, a group I never expected to join so early in life. I expected to be feeling sad, but I was in too much shock, I had so much to organize.

What surprises me now, is that heart conditions are not just something that happens to the elderly. Despite almost loosing track of the appointments I have had with my cardiologist, I have yet to be in the waiting room with anyone even close to my age. It's a stark reminder that many people my age, don't realize that they have a heart condition until it's too late. Within a week of my diagnosis, I was told of two people under 50 who died suddenly from Cardiomyopathy.

Their stories haunted me, they were happy living their life, until it was to late, leaving young children all alone. The symptoms early on are hard to pick up, and for some people there are very few symptoms. They had no warning, no visible sign, both just passed suddenly, and after the fact in autopsy, they were diagnosed with Cardiomyopathy. Recently a fit healthy man in his early 50's a marathon runner past away whilst on holidays, and in his autopsy they realised he had an enlarged heart.

Cardiomyopathy can be silent, creeping up on you without the usual alarms that make you go see a doctor. For so many, the symptoms are subtle or not at all, blending into the background noise of daily life, easily dismissed as just being tired, fatigued or out of shape.

For me without my watch, I would have put it down to a busy life, and being 'a bit unfit'. Who doesn't get out of breath when exercising? Who isn't tired at the end of the day? Especially when raising young children. Being tired, out of breathe, fatigued are all things we all experience at some stage, but sometimes they're not as harmless as we think.

The words go round and round in your mind, Cardiomyopathy, Ventricular Bigeminy, 3-year life expectancy, 5 years if I was lucky, and did I feel lucky, a 30 year old with a heart condition, not really. Forty one thousand PVC's (Premature ventricular contractions) recorded from the halter monitor in only 24 hours which meant 41% of my beats were irregular. You realise that in all the shock there are so many things that you should have asked, but shock does strange things to you.

How do you even begin to process the news that you could be dead in three years, that you have to allow a cardiologist to operate on your heart, to even have a chance at survival? The thoughts swirled, and the gravity of it all sank in slowly. What do you tell the kids? Do you even tell them?

How do you explain to them that their mom's heart, something they've always taken for granted as strong and steady, something that cares and loves for them so deeply, is suddenly the very thing that could fail her? The heart that beats for them, is now a source of such uncertainty and fear.

I felt the weight of responsibility as a mother to protect them, shield them from the harsh reality of what we are facing, to model resilience, but to protect them from the harsh reality of my diagnosis, but also the need to be truthful with them. My thoughts swirled I couldn't hide the inevitable operation from them, but they didn't need to know the full severity of the condition.

As I grappled with the overwhelming thoughts, I was aware of the delicate balance between vulnerability and strength, and I made a choice, the same choice I had made many times,

I was going to be strong for my children, for my husband, they didn't need to see me crumble under the weight of fear. I would continue to push through, to be strong for them.

The Diagnosis

Now I need to start with I am not a Doctor, so this is my interpretation of my diagnosis, do not use any of this as actual medical information. Now that is out there, the one thing I need to mention with specialist doctors is to ask questions, once the shock wore off I realized I hadn't asked many questions about my diagnosis, so was left to make a follow-up with my amazing GP and ask him for more information.

So my diagnosis was two-fold

Ventricular Bigeminy

In layman's terms, it is an irregular heartbeat, not just one here or there, but when you have an irregular heartbeat between each of your normal heartbeats. So when I thought my heart rate was 35, it wasn't, it was still around 70, but only 35 were doing their job, putting an undue strain on my heart.

Also means, when my heart rate was sitting at 80-90 it was actually beating between 160-180 beats per minute.

Cardiomyopathy

For those who get this diagnosis, I advise you; don't search this online, it will do nothing to ease your anxiety. The term breaks down.

Cardio means Heart

Myo means muscle

Pathy means disease or disorder

So bottom line Cardiomyopathy is a disease of the heart muscle.

There are three different types of Cardiomyopathy,

1. **Dilated cardiomyopathy**

2. **Hypertrophic cardiomyopathy**

3. **Restrictive cardiomyopathy**

I was diagnosed with **Dilated Cardiomyopathy**

Dilated cardiomyopathy means that your heart is enlarged and as it grows bigger, the walls of the heart stretch. It makes it harder for your body to pump blood around the body and can lead to heart failure, as it compromises the heart's ability to pump normally.

I was told by my cardiologist, that my two diagnoses are a bit like the Chicken and the egg analogy. Sometimes Dilated cardiomyopathy causes, Ventricular Bigeminy, or sometimes it's the other way around.

Now we were praying that it was the irregular heartbeats (Ventricular Bigeminy) that was causing my heart to work too hard and causing it to get enlarged as if that was the case and they could stop the irregular heartbeats there was a good chance they could stop the Heart from becoming even more damaged, and hopefully, then the heart would shrink back in size.

But only time would tell, first I would need to have the operation and then wait.

9th March 2021

I would never imagined that I would be lying in the hospital by myself waiting for heart surgery. Truthfully four weeks earlier I wouldn't have even imagined that I would be getting heart surgery. But even then when my cardiologist had told me about my surgery, I imagined it differently, I expected to be waiting with Scott having him beside me offering reassurance.

Covid and Covid restrictions stole a lot of things from people, especially in regards to healthcare, and as I was waiting for surgery I was feeling the brunt of it. However it was such a mixed feeling, I felt blessed that I was able to have the surgery, as many other states had been cancelling operations due to the pandemic. I understood the fragility of the situation, the risks that the country was facing, and I was so thankful that I didn't have to postpone my surgery.

I waited in the foyer of the hospital alone, feeling my heart beat in my chest, I looked at the low heart rate notification on my phone hoping that I wouldn't have to see that alert ever again. My husband had dropped me off, however, no-one else except patients were allowed in the hospital until recovery, which meant the long wait for the surgery I would have to do alone. Sure I felt it, but I felt it more for my husband, stuck outside waiting. Waiting for the call that I was going in, waiting for the call that the operation was finished, waiting to hear that I was safe, just waiting.

After what seemed like an eternity a nurse called my name. We walk down the corridor, both masked up, quiet, no small talk I feel my nervousness growing with each step closer to the Surgery ward.

I walked into the empty room, the air thick with antiseptic, there was a robe sitting folded on the chair, a large bag to put my clothes into, and a sterile hospital bed. There was space for multiple people however due to covid restrictions, I was alone.

They hook me up to the heart monitor and tell me that 50% of my beats are now PVCs. In the space of four weeks, they had gone up another 9% from 41%, which means my heart is having to work harder and harder each day. I shudder to think if I had waited any longer, how much more damage I would have done.

They make me do another COVID test, and even though the whole family had negative Covid results, the the day before, I vividly remember how nervous I was as I waited for the results. I didn't want anything to stop the operation from happening. My Mum had flown down from Cairns, Scott's parents were parked in our front lawn in their Caravan. My twin sister had flown up from Ballarat, too many things had fallen into place for this operation to have anything stop it now. The results came back negative, relief washed over me, the operation was going ahead.

Memory fascinates me, Thankfully I wrote lots of notes, as some memories are hazy, however, I still vividly remember the room that I was in as waited for surgery, I was by myself lying there waiting for what felt like hours, No awkward chit-chat whilst you wait, just alone with your thoughts. I still vividly remember the checkerboard tiles on the roof, stark and cold, as I lay there alone, waiting for the operation.

I remember My thoughts swaying toward my four amazing children, I wanted to be around to help them and see them grow up, this operation had to work as I needed to be there for them. They still need me. I thought of my husband, who was sitting at home waiting for news, and my heart ached with the weight of uncertainty that lay ahead.

Even now years on I realize I never had a chance to worry about my own fears and anxieties. My focus was on my children, and my husband that's who I needed to be strong for. But in that sterile room, as I waited by myself, my thoughts broken occasionally by the hospital sounds, I had moments to think. To think about life and its fragility, Life was forcing me to confront my mortality and thoughts that I didn't want to face in my 30s.

I had read all about the cardiac ablation, and how I was going to have a twilight anaesthesia, which I was the most nervous about. Supposedly I would still be awake for the procedure, however most likely would not remember it afterwards, it funny I was more nervous about being awake for the procedure than for the doctor purposely creating scar tissue in my heart.

Finally, the door opened and the nurse came in, It was time. As they wheeled me into the operating room, I looked around at the medical staff, my life was in their hands, I closed my eyes, and took a deep breath there was no going back now.

As I sat in the room, I found solace in the small things, the soft beeping of the machines, the gentle conversations between the doctors, nurses and technicians in the rooms. Each sound was a reminder, that I was in capable hands.

In the final moments I wandered how much I would remember and the next thing I was back in my room in recovery, the world slowly coming back into focus.

I had made it through the surgery, now I would have to wait and see if it had worked.

One Night

I don't know if it was because of COVID, or if it was just the usual procedure, but I was told as long as I recovered well, I would only need to spend one night in the hospital, and then I could go home.

After the operation, I was instructed to lie flat for 6 hours to make sure that I didn't cause any damage or excessive bleeding to the wound in my groin, and then would have to take it easy at home for a while. It was amazing to think that the tiny little incision, that seemed so far away from my heart was how they had performed the hopeful lifesaving surgery.

Due to COVID there was strict restrictions on Visitors in the hospital. For children under twelve there was no restrictions in place and our youngest two could have visited me, however, the older two had to be vaccinated to visit the ward, and ironically at that time COVID vaccination hadn't been approved for children who were 12-15 years old so it was a funny spot to be in, they couldn't come in if they weren't vaccinated, however, they also weren't old enough to be vaccinated. We made the decision that it wasn't fair to bring in just the younger two, so they all stayed home instead.

We had plenty going on at home anyway, with my twin sister, mum at our house, and Scott's parents camped out in our front yard in a caravan. somehow whilst I was in hospital, a plastic breadboard had made its way into our oven and had melted into everything.

So whilst I recovered quietly in the hospital room, I received hilarious photos, of my once pristine oven, that was now a sticky mess of melted plastic, trying to work out how it could have ever happened. I was once again thankful that my mum and sister were there helping clean and pull it all apart.

A night in the cardio ward felt strangely similar to a hospital emergency ward, with constant noise, bright lights, and staff coming and going at all times of the night, whilst I was thankful to be in a private room, it didn't help with the constant noise and interruptions, so I was very happy when my cardiologist popped in early the next morning and told me that he could already see an improvement in my heart, and If I could get up and show them I could walking around gently and they would discharge me later that morning. I was under strict instructions to take it easy for the next four weeks, I would have to learn to stop and let others help me.

Thankfully he warned me that I would experience mild to moderate chest pain or tightness, as well as pain where the incision was made, so when the painkiller wore off and my chest began to feel tight I didn't feel panicked. I looked over at my discharge paperwork, with an appointment time to pick up another halter monitor four weeks later to see if the PVC's had stopped, but I knew I would have to wait 3 months to see if my EF (Ejection fracture) had gone up, only then would we know if the operation was a success.

Whilst I was happy to hear this news, I also wished that Scott could be here to talk to the Cardiologist, so he to could hear the cautious optimism in the doctors voice, but instead, I would have to pass the news on through text messages and phone calls until he arrived to pick me up.

Scott came to pick me up later that morning, and we made our way home in silence, both of us lost in thought. It was strange how something so life-altering could happen, yet life outside the hospital walls continued on as usual.

The kids were at home, eagerly to see me, and whilst I couldn't wait to be back in the comfort of our home, I also felt the weight of everything that had happened press down on me. The kids didn't know the seriousness of the situation, they knew that something was wrong with my heart and that I had to have a small operation to fix it.

As we pulled into the driveway, I paused staring at the caravan parked in the front yard, cars crowding everywhere, before I even walked in the door, you could hear the sounds of laughter greeting me, but something felt different. I wasn't just coming home from an ordinary appointment, I was coming home with a new sense of fragility, a heightened awareness that my body had limits now, and I'd need to listen carefully to it, something I had never done before.

The kids rushed towards me, the younger ones eager to hug me, even though we'd prepared them to be gentle and careful, the older two much more aware and more cautious in their approach. Their excitement made me smile, but all the adults quickly reminded them that I needed to rest. My mum and sister greeted me with concerned looks, checking in on how I was feeling, and I reassured them with a faint smile that I was fine, as I headed straight upstairs back into bed.

As the day wore on, I settled into my new but temporary routine. Resting in bed, the kids coming in and out to visit as I watched TV, monitoring my heart rate with the Apple Watch, thankful for the ECG function that my version of the Apple watch has, and trying not to get to worried about whether the operation had been successful. The house downstairs kept moving around me, but I was sitting quietly upstairs.

But despite the noise and movement, I couldn't shake the feeling that things were different now. I wasn't invincible. None of us were. I was aware now of the vulnerability that came with each heart beat, and that realization had left a mark, one that would continue to linger even after the surgery incisions and discomfort would heal.

April 2021

The month that followed the operation felt like an eternity. Each day seemed to stretch out endlessly as I waited for the follow-up appointment and my next 24-hour heart monitor to find out how the operation had gone. I wasn't allowed to exercise, couldn't even help much with the housework. I had to stop and rest something that I had never really done before, it was strange to me. With four children we were still at the stage when you didn't even stop on holidays, so after a couple of weeks I was getting stir crazy, and even though I wanted to break the rules, there was no way my husband was going to let me.

I was so thankful that my mum and twin sister had been able to fly up and be with our family over the time of the operation, but my sister had flown back home and life was getting back to normal for everyone but me, normal life had to happen, kids had school, appointments, and it was hard for me to let mum and Scott help me, and to stop and rest. Finally, four weeks later, I found myself once again, hooked up to the monitor, this time whilst familiar it held a higher weight. This time I knew the stakes, if it hadn't worked, the clock would be ticking down. But I also felt hopeful, that things had improved.

Finally four weeks later, it was time to face the results again. This time there was no boxes to unpack, no furniture to move, so I went about my day feeding the kids, tagging along as Scott drove kids to after school appointments, I went for a short walk so that the monitor would see what happens. I tried to keep myself positive, I hadn't received a low heart rate notification since the day of the surgery, and every ECG I had done on the apple watch had come up ok, surely that was a good sign. But the question remained was it the operation that was working, or the heart medication I was taking every day that was helping? Once again though I would have to wait, this time though it was only a few days to look over the data.

The morning of the follow-up appointment arrived, and I could hardly contain my nervousness as I walked into the office. I was bracing myself for the news, whatever it might be. The cardiologist had reviewed the results, I held Scott's hand tightly, looking over at him, and as the cardiologist spoke, I could hardly believe what I was hearing.

The monitor had recorded zero premature ventricular contractions (PVCs) over the full 24 hours—a result that was nothing short of a relief. The words "Operation success" felt like a weight was beginning to be lifted off my shoulders. My heart was finally showing signs of stability. Of course there where still many lingering questions, ones that would take years to answer, would the PVCs come back, would my heart heal and begin to shrink and begin to function again correctly, would my blood pressure stabilize?

Whilst those questions were important and real, so to was the hope that was starting to come back again for the first time in months.

April 14, 2021, became a turning point. The operation had been successful, and the fears that had loomed over me for the past months were replaced with cautious optimism. The road to recovery was still ahead, but for now, the results were a beacon of hope, proving that sometimes, against the odds, things can indeed get better.

14th June 2021

As I walked into my follow up appointment only two months later, I felt a wave of nervousness wash over me. It struck me that before my appointment only 6 months earlier, I hadn't even noticed my heart was failing. How then could I trust that I would know my heart was improving when I didn't realize anything was wrong in the first place? I was nervous, I had been praying that the lack of PVC's would mean that my heart was shrinking, that my heart function was improving but until after the echo (echocardiogram) I really had no idea.

As I lay on the exam bed, the radiographer pushed the cold ultrasound gel over my chest, I am sure to her I looked calm, casually asking her questions about her family, when inside I was wishing I knew what the measurements meant. Was my heart shrinking, was I improving? Her face was calm, showing no signs of anything, no worry, no happiness, just studious, careful measurements, but I studied every look, every minor adjustment of the ultrasound wand, every glance at the monitor, the small creases of her brow, hoping for a positive sign, a flicker of reassurance.

Every now and then, her gaze would flicker from the monitor as she repositioned the ultrasound wand. Her face gave nothing away, completely neutral, her expression focused on the task at hand. She was experienced at this, not just the echo, but the worried patients that came in too. There was no visible concern, but also no hint of reassurance. I hoped she would say something, anything, but she was professional, kind, but not showing any recognition good or bad.

As she pressed the wand a little harder into my chest, capturing more measurements, I found myself holding my breath. I wanted to ask her outright, "Is my heart getting smaller? Am I improving? Do you see any changes?" But I knew she wouldn't be able to give me those answers. Not yet, that was not her job, not her responsibility.

The seconds felt like minutes, every pause in her movements making my mind question what it all meant. After what felt like an eternity, she finished, handing me a towel to wipe the gel off. She offered me a polite smile but said nothing about the results. "Your doctor will go over everything with you soon," she said, her voice as neutral as her expression had been.

I nodded, thanking her, but inside, the uncertainty gnawed at me. I got dressed, This was just another step in the process, I reminded myself. Answers were coming, and with them, hopefully, good news.

Sitting in the waiting room again, the wait felt like an eternity, finally the Cardiologist walks out of his room, he smiles a reassuring smile and calls my name. I look over at Scott, I would never again walk into the cardiologist office alone I had learnt from my mistake.

After a brief exchange of pleasantries, the cardiologist looks at me with a reassuring smile. "Your heart is heading in the right direction," he said. "The irregular heartbeats you were experiencing are still completely gone."

I let out a sigh of relief until that moment I don't think I realised I had been holding my breathe, He continued, "When we first started, your ejection fraction (EF) was quite low, around 37-45%. After today I can confirm, it's at 60%. That's a significant improvement and indicates that your heart function is back to where it should be."

I nodded, absorbing the information. My husband asked, "What about the enlargement of her heart?"

"Your heart was previously classified as 35% enlarged," he explained, "but now it's only 17% enlarged. That's a major reduction and shows that your heart is recovering well, however, it is still larger than we would like."

He glanced at my medication list and noted, "We need to continue your medication, and hopefully it will continue to shrink. This is a positive sign that your condition is improving, and hopefully, when we come back in 9 months it will have continued to improve."

My heart swelled with relief and gratitude. "So, what does this mean for my daily life?"

"You've been cleared to start to try a live a normal life again, it is time to get back to gentle exercise, go start walking again, start gentle exercise, your heart rate can't go above 160 beats per minute. So make sure you keep track of it," he said. "As long as your heart continues to stay at this size or smaller, Your life expectancy is now expected to be normal. This is a huge improvement from where we started."

I couldn't help but smile, feeling a weight lifted off my shoulders. "And what's next?"

"You'll have a follow-up appointment with me in nine months, as well as regular appointments with your GP" he said. "You need to stay on your heart medication for the foreseeable future, but I am hopeful it will continue to improve.

I look down at the Apple watch, the thing that alerted me to my heart rate in the first place, and smile. Even now it will be important for my recovery, and getting back into exercise.

With that, we left the office filled with a little more hope and optimism. The journey wasn't over, but the path ahead suddenly looked brighter.

Fear

It's only now as I look back that I realized how deeply Fear had began to take hold on my life through the recovery process. When Dr Chee told me "to keep my heart rate under 160" he gave me a figure, something concrete to measure. But with that number became an invisible weight, it gave Fear something to hold onto.

Back before my diagnosis exercise was hopeful, there was something so relaxing and calming about long walks along the beach, as the cold water lapped at my feet. Weekend hikes through the national park where you would push yourself almost to exhaustion but feel exhilirated at the end. Back then, my heart rate was the last thing on my mind. I was more focused on how many kms the exercise tracker on my Apple watch said that I had walked, making sure that if it was sitting a few hundreds shy of the next km, I would push myself just a little bit further so it would clock over to the next km.

Even in the first few months of my diagnosis it was easy, I hadn't allowed myself time to fear... fear the diagnosis, fear the prognosis, however the minute I had that number, **160 beats**, the target, fear latched on. My mind became fixated on that 160, so every time I exercised and felt my heartbeat quicken I would look down at my watch, the minute my heart rate would begin to climb from 140... 145 I would feel my intensity drop. Fear would begin creeping in. I would slow down, stop, and take a break, not because my body was failing, but because I was letting fear win.

"Slow down," Fear would whisper in my ear, "Take it easy, slow down"

One morning, Scott and I went to an exercise class together, I laced up my shoes, feeling hopeful, ready to exercise, but only minutes in to the 45 minute class, I looked at my watch, the numbers began ticking up quickly 135, 140, 145, 150. My breathe became faster, not from the exercise but from the growing anxiety building in my chest. I slowed between the sets of exercise, my intensity dropping, maybe It was too early, maybe I should sit it out. My mind raced. I remember back to before the diagnosis and how my only thoughts were about pushing through the pain, now I was having to push through my own fear.

To everyone else though I stayed stoic, calm

and composed, the strong one, that once again didn't need any help. No one else could see my thoughts, could see fear sinking in. When people would ask how I was going, I would just say "Great, just slowly easing back into it." My family bought it, but they always have. I was the strong one, I didn't need any help. I never did. They didn't hear the silent negotiations I made with myself every time I exercised, every time I would go for that walk, or even lace up my shoes for gentle exercise. I was a silent prisoner to my own thoughts.

Fear wasn't just a feeling anymore; it was a physical presence, living in my chest right alongside my heartbeat. It dictated my movements, whispered limits into my ear, and made every exercise session feel like added pressure. I began to anticipate the moment my heart rate would approach 160.

Better slow down, you don't want to reach 160.

I would brace myself for the imagined consequences. Consequences I hadn't even been told about.

I didn't share any of this to anyone, as I couldn't add that pressure onto others, they had their own thoughts and fears to contend with. So each day, I let fear keep pressing its invisible weight on me, one quiet heartbeat at a time.

March 2022

I walked into the cardiologist's office in March 2022, nine months had passed since I had been in his office and I was hopeful for another round of good news.

Another echocardiogram had been done, and I was hopeful that my heart had continued to shrink, the medication I was on whilst important did seem to make me feel a little lethargic at times, and I had seen my weight keep going up, whether that was a side effect of the medication, the limited exercise or just the stress of the last few years I wasnt sure.

As we sat down, I looked at my husband again, and the cardiologist looked through the latest echocardiogram results, I watched his face closely, as he did calculations on his calculator. His expression was neutral and focused and the minutes dragged on.

"Well," he said, glancing up from the papers, "there's no change. I was hopeful that after another nine months, your heart would continue to shrink, but it is still 17% larger than it should be. "

I blinked, trying to process it. No improvement after all this time? I had now spent a whole year without caffeine, I had spent the last nine months lowering my risk and taking my medication diligently. Yet here I was, my heart showing no further signs of improvement, despite everything.

"What does that mean?" I asked.

He hesitated for a moment before responding. "It's good news, your heart hasn't got any worse, it has stayed the same, and whilst we would have preferred it to keep shrinking, stability is great news, your blood pressure is 110/70. Your heart looks strong. So its time we reduce your medication," he said, "and hopefully your heart will continue to stay the same size.

The words hung in the air like a weight. Cut back on medication? It felt counterintuitive, like giving up on progress. But he explained that continuing at full dosage wasn't necessary anymore since my heart wasn't responding. Now, it was a waiting game—monitoring, hoping the condition wouldn't deteriorate.

I had one final question to ask him, the one that my daughter had thought was the most important. "Am I able to go on roller coasters now?"

For the first time, I heard my cardiologist laugh—a real, hearty belly laugh that seemed to catch him off guard. "I have never been asked that question before, and I don't think I ever will," he said, his laughter lingering as he shook his head in disbelief. The sound of his amusement filled the room, lightening the atmosphere in a way I hadn't expected.

I thought back to the waiting room, filled with patients all pushing 70, their faces marked by years and experience, and smiled, fully understanding his reaction.

"Yes," he finally said, his voice still warm with humor, "your heart is steady; I am happy for you to go on rollercoasters."

As I left the office, a mixture of frustration and uncertainty settled in. No change. No difference. I wasn't getting worse, but I wasn't getting better either. And now, all I could do was hope that my heart wouldn't turn in the wrong direction.

A Reminder

April 2022, two years since my father passed away. You would think that with what happened with Dad I would have learned something from his passing, that it would have caused me to rush quickly when something seemed wrong with my health, but the fact I waited 6 months with repeated low heart notifications shows that as people we are the same, we fall into the same patterns, even when we should know better.

My Dad had signs of a stroke on the night of the 7th of March, he was out with his Mates, and they noticed something was wrong, so they urged him to go to the Hospital. He listened at first and made his way to the hospital. But upon arrival he changed his mind, he decided it could wait, the line was too long, and the room was too noisy, so he went home to sleep it off. After all, he convinced himself it wasn't a big deal.

But by the next morning, it was too late, and he had what doctors described as a catastrophic stroke, 3/4 of the left side of his brain was affected. The part of the brain that affects both his receptive and expressive language, he would survive another month, but the damage was done, apart from half a dozen words, the colorful, larger-than-life character of my childhood was no more.

We convince ourselves it won't happen to us, that the medical test, the decision can wait, but ultimately sometimes they can't.

You see my first low heart rate notification happened on 10th April the day before my Dad passed away, you would think that knowing what happened to Dad, seeing him lying there first hand, it would have prompted me to be more vigilant with my health. That I would be more aware of what was going on, that it would have made me ask questions, Made me book in to my doctor at the first sign of trouble, however, we do not always learn from the past.

It took six months of low heart notifications from my Apple Watch for me to finally take action. I looked back on the records, and some days I had over 9 alerts, but still I did nothing. Each time it buzzed, it was a subtle reminder, a subtle warning that my heart wasn't working as it should, but I brushed it off. I had so many excuses. I was too busy, there was something more important, someone more important, something that could delay that all-important doctor's visit. Looking back, it was frightening how easily I could ignore the signs. And yet, people do it every day.

It's something I will have to live with for the rest of my life. Despite all the positives I've gained from this journey, my heart remains significantly larger than it should be. Cardiomyopathy, a condition that will always be a part of me.

You see the truth is, we always think we have time. We always believe that these things happen to other people, not to us. Until they do.

It makes me think about my children, and how much they still need me. And I wondered, if I hadn't come in when I did, would I have ended up like my Dad? A statistic, Waiting too long, convincing myself that it wasn't serious until it was too late?

There's a strange comfort in routines, even when they're harmful. We settle into habits, into patterns, because they feel familiar. Sometimes though we need to push past the familiar and the easy, Sometimes things need to change. I couldn't keep ignoring the signs—not anymore.

We convince ourselves it won't happen to us. That the medical test, the decision, and the action can wait. But sometimes, it can't.

13th September 2022

There is something to be said, about feeling like you have hit rock bottom, and realising that you had only just hit a ledge on the way down.

I can vividly remember where I was when the make shift ledge I had landed on, collapsed under me in spectacular fashion, as a parent it is one thing to deal with your own health issues, but when something happens to your children it hits you differently. We were just beginning to heal from the last two years, and starting to feel like our world was beginning to improve, I was driving home along the Sunshine Motorway at the start of the three roundabouts that you go through as you enter Noosaville, when Scott called panic in his voice.

"Jacqui has had a seizure" he said.

My world stopped once again, shock permeated through my whole body. A seizure, only two days ago, we had celebrated her 17th birthday, and now she was having a seizure.

I drove, fast towards home, Thankful I had just reached the part of the motorway where it split into two lanes, so I didn't have to sit slow behind other drivers. Each minute passing my mind began to think, what had caused the seizure, was it a reaction to the medication she had recently started to treat the side effects of ross river and COVID that was plaguing her body, or was it a sign of something more sinister.

As a parent, you're hardwired to protect your children, to shield them from pain and danger. But in that moment, I didn't only feel powerless, I was powerless. Fear began wrapping itself around me, its grip unrelenting. The only thing I could do was pray, pray that the paramedics would come soon, pray that they would find an answer, pray that she would be alright, and pray that Scott and I would have the strength to get through the next challenge that faced us.

My thoughts then began circling to the practicalities of life, our son, was working in town, at his first job, who would go pick him up, would we have to wake the little two up, and drag them from their beds, as they couldn't be left home alone. Every question felt like a lifeline, something to keep my mind thinking of the practicalities, rather than drowning in the unbearable unknown. I clung to these thoughts as if solving them would delay the inevitable reality that was waiting for me when I walked through the door.

When I finally arrived home, Jacqui had just finished her seizure. She was lying still, her breathing shallow as we waited for the paramedics. She was confused a common side effect after a seizure, they call it the postictal state, but for someone who has never seen it before. It's heartbreaking, my heart was racing, and for someone who prides herself in being calm under pressure, I was anything but.

The facade of composure I usually wore had completely crumbled, leaving me raw and exposed, the one time my husband has said he saw me completely panicked, unsure if I was doing enough or even the right thing to help her. Each passing second felt like an eternity, stretching out the helplessness in ways I could hardly bear. Seeing her like that was something that simultaneously filled me with relief, relief she was alive, but dread as I didn't know what was happening.

I sat beside her, trying to offer whatever comfort I could, and then, before the paramedics had arrived, I heard a guttural sound, a sound that only people who have witnessed a seizure themselves will recognise. Another seizure had begun. Hearing about one is one thing, but witnessing it is something else entirely. The violent jerking, the unnatural stillness afterward it's an image that you can never forget I was powerless, all I could say was "It's going to be ok, because it had to be" this was my daughter, she was innocent, she was a child.

Community is a powerful thing, we had no family in Queensland, and in the past, that would have made it extremely hard to deal with what came next, even having to navigate picking up our son from work, but we had made friends with amazing neighbours, and as soon as the ambulance pulled up, they had come around to make sure we were ok, they sat in our house whilst our younger two slept blissfully unaware of all the commotion downstairs, I went in the ambulance, and Scott went to pick up our son, so he could hear about it from a Parent.

The Paramedics were amazing, calm talking to me and Jacqui, even in her postictal confusion, they talked to her, reassured her, explained things to her. We arrived at the hospital and they rushed us into the resus bay, as she had never had a seizure before they needed to work out why it was happening, and make sure she would be safe it it happened again.

We arrive at the hospital about 9pm and settle in for a long night of tests, but in between the wait, the tests, there was light, she has fun talking to the nurses about Disney, her favourite thing, another nurse started talking to her about her favourite vlogs. It's the little things that bring joy as you wait in a hospital ward. In between the conversation, the tests, Jacqui would drift in and out of both confusion and sleep. But I couldn't sleep, between the busy noises, and the constant worry, I sat in the upright chair, watching every monitor.

But as the night wore on, I begun to relax, my eyes became heavy and I began to try and get a little sleep, and then suddenly at 2am it happens again, before I can even call out, multiple nurses are here, they put on an oxygen mask, they move her into a better position, I watch, relief flooding over me, I am so happy that we are in the hospital and we are not alone, when this is happening.

A few hours later they move us into the Neuro ward, and we settle in for the next couple of days, she continues to have test, multiple EEGs, both sleep deprived, and when she is more conscious, we sit with the doctors once again my heart begins to pound loudly.

"We have found some abnormalities, she has IGE (Idiopathic generalized epilepsy) and GGE (Genetic generalized epilepsies), later this would be further explained as juvenile myoclonic epilepsy, the random movements, that we had talked to multiple doctors about, the 'tick' like movements, they had tried to explain away as related to her Autism, was actually myoclonic seizures, my heart broke to think, that the signs had been missed for years.

But right there in the hospital room, I felt an odd mix of emotion. There was a real sense of relief that we had an answer, when they say knowledge is power, they are right, with the diagnosis, we could make a plan. But then the worry set in, this was her new normal, she was about to go for her license, but now she would have to wait six months before she could drive. She would never go swimming on her own again, epilepsy brings with it a new set of challenges.

The day finally came to take her home. Stepping back through the front door, everything felt the same, yet nothing felt normal.

Jacqui was tired, but she couldn't sleep in her own room, The thought of sleep filled her with dread. What if it happened again? What if this time, she didn't wake up. We moved a mattress into our room, and the next few nights sleep was hard to come by for all of us.

But then I looked at my arm, my Apple watch, what if this could help us? I began to research and found that there were apps out there, that would alert others if a seizure was happening, so about a week after her seizure she went to bed in her own room, with her own apple watch on her arm.

It was a small device, but it brought us an incredible sense of security. Knowing that it could monitor her movements and send alerts if something happened allowed us all to sleep a little easier. The watch didn't just symbolize hope; it became an essential tool in her care going forward, bridging the gap between fear and freedom. It gave Jacqui the confidence to reclaim small pieces of her independence, and for me, as her parent, it was a reminder of how technology can transform lives in the most unexpected ways.

Another Journey

Each health challenge you face as a Family, or as a person, is its own unique journey. And whilst I would love to share more, that is not my story to tell. Even now as I write this book, Jacqui story is still ongoing.

As a family, there are times when you begin to feel like you are getting on top of things, finding your rhythm, feeling in control. But then, without warning, epilepsy rears its head, and you feel like you are falling back down further than before.

Every new seizure is terrifying. It's not just the physical toll that it takes, but the emotional weight of never knowing when or where she will be when it strikes. It's so easy to fall back into fear, fear of the unknown, fear of what comes next. it reminds me of my heart condition that was lurking silently ready to strike, their is no warning and it makes you feel like you are falling through the dark without a safety ledge to hold onto.

Both journey's as a patient and as a Parent are unpredictable, filled with moments when you feel completely powerless.

However with each new medication, each adjustment, you have to hold onto a slither of hope. Hope that the doctors will find the correct medication, the correct treatment. Hope that one day she will here the words you are waiting for yourself, "Everything looks stable". It's that hope that helps you push through each day.

Resilence isn't about never falling down, its about finding the strength to rise again, every time, as the future is worth it. It's holding onto faith that no matter how dark it feels at the time, there is always a glimmer of light to look at, to propel you forward.

Just like my journey with my heart, the journey isn't linear, some days feel like progress, and you feel like you are climbing slowly up out of the hole, and others are a never ending setback, pulling you back deeper into fear, and frustration.

But resilence isn't about pretending everything is okay but understanding sometimes life is hard and it feels impossible, but choosing to move forward anyway. Because the truth is every little step forward, no matter how small matters, and get's you closer to the future.

Everytime you choose hope over fear, everytime you pick yourself up after a fall, your proving that Life is worth it. The future holds a promise of brighter days ahead.

Follow Up

February 2023

Twelve months had gone by quickly so many things had happened in our life, here I found myself once again sitting in the cardiologist's waiting room. This time, though, the feeling was different. The pressure was even higher now, I felt like it was even more important to get good news. Our family needed some good news.

I could hear my heart beating steadily in my

chest, a calm, rhythmic thud that felt reassuring, unlike the erratic beats that had plagued me two years earlier.

This was it, the moment that would tell me if all the treatments, tests, and lifestyle changes had worked. Was everything still as it should be? Had my heart truly healed?

I glanced down at my watch, my constant companion for the past two years. It had been more than just a tool for telling time, it had become my safety net. Whenever doubts or fears crept in, I'd press the crown and let the watch perform a basic ECG. Each time, it had shown a clear rhythm, steady and strong. But today felt different. Today wasn't about the watch giving me a brief reassurance; today was the real test.

I felt a mixture of hope and nerves building up inside me. My resting heart rate was steady now, something I hadn't been able to say for a long time, but there was always that lingering "what if." I shifted in my chair and glanced at the corridor, waiting for the cardiologist to call my name.

The wait felt longer than usual, or maybe it was just my anticipation making every second stretch out. I had come so far—my EF (ejection fraction) had jumped from a worrisome 37–45% to a much healthier 60%. My heart, which had once been 35% enlarged, had now shrunk to only 17% enlarged. All signs pointed to success, but I needed to hear it from him, to feel that weight lifted.

When we finally made our way into his office, I sat up a little straighter, bracing myself for whatever news he was about to deliver.

"There have been no major changes in the last twelve months, even with twelve months of the medication, your heart has stayed the same, whilst we were hopeful that the medication would bring a further changes, it is still positive". he paused.

I exhaled slowly. Stability wasn't the dramatic improvement I had been hoping for, but it was still a win. It meant my heart hadn't worsened.

He went on to explain that because everything was stable, we could now cut my medication dosage in half. It was a cautious approach, easing off the meds while monitoring closely to make sure nothing deteriorated.

"I'm confident that you can live a completely normal life," he said. "But we'll keep an eye on things, I need you to come back in six months for another stress test and echo cardiogram.

The relief washed over me, but there was still that lingering caution. Cutting back on medication felt like a risk, even though he assured me it was the right move. My heart wasn't getting worse, but it wasn't getting any better either.

As I left the office, the weight I'd been carrying for so long felt lighter—but not completely gone. It wasn't the perfect ending I had imagined, but it was still hope. My life, as it seemed, could go on as normal, and for now, that was more than enough.

Being Thankful

There are so many things that I am thankful for as I look back at my journey with my heart. Some of them seem small, and at the time inconsequential. But they have all had such an impact on my life.

To begin with I am so thankful that my husband bought me an Apple watch, something I initially thought was just a fun gadget something to tell the time on, but without it I truly believe I wouldn't be here anymore.

I am so thankful that even though it took me over six months to heed the warnings, I did eventually listen.

More importantly though, I owe so much to my husband and my mum, without their gentle encouragement, making me accountable, urging me to make that crucial appointment. The warnings on my watch would have been for nothing, and my health would have continued deteriorating.

Most of all though, I am thankful that I went to a doctor, that listened, That made the difference, he took the time to listen, make the phone calls and book me in to the specialist required. I am thankful for our medical system that at times might be flawed, still gives everyone the opportunity to get the care we require.

I am thankful for amazing advancements in medical care. There have been many times over my life where I have been thankful to live in modern times, but even more when we think that many of the medical techniques, the medicines the cardiologist used to help repair the damage have only been around for 30-40 years.

Back in in the 1980's Doctors would begin to start performing this operation, however the first cardiac ablation specifically for atrial fibrillation wasn't even performed until 1990, the very operation that would one day save my life.

Like many medical procedures, the innovation and skill behind cardiac ablation is astounding. The procedure itself involves inserting a thin, flexible tube called a catheter into a blood vessel, mine was through my groin. My skilled cardiologist then had to carefully navigate it into the heart, where it delivered energy to specific areas that was causing the irregular electrical signals. This energy zapped the problematic areas, hoping to help restore a normal heartbeat. When I went in I was told that there was chance they wouldn't be able to find the part of the heart that was causing issues.

The idea that such a delicate and intricate procedure could have been conceived and perfected in just a few decades to be is miraculous, and it makes me wonder what else will modern medicine perfect and conceive over the next ten, twenty years.

28th August 2023

August 2023 arrived, and with it, another appointment, twelve months since my last check-up. As I sat once again in the cardiologist's office, I looked at my feet, I had forgotten I was supposed to do a stress test, and I had arrived in sandals not a great start to the appointment. I glanced at my watch, I didn't have time to go home and get my sneakers so I would have to run barefoot.

I glance again at my watch, as I had so many times before, but this time not out of fear but habit. The steady rhythm of my heart had become a source of comfort, the daily ECGs I used to do with my Apple watch, had become weekly, then fortnightly as my confidence in my heart grew. But everytime I walked into the office, I start to think, have I missed something?

They called my name and I took my sandals off and wandered in, this time I felt ready to do my next stress test, aware of what I was about to face.

I completed my stress test, this time though the test seemed to drag on, I went up level by level, part of me was thankful that he didn't stop me quickly, I took it as a sign that my heart was improving, but the whole time the cardiologist watched over my shoulder, his expression was neutral, causing me to second guess my thoughts.

When we went through the test results, it too was neutral just like his expression, no bad news, but no clear good news either. He sat down across from us, glancing through my charts and test results, just like he had twelve months earlier.

"Well," he began, his voice measured, "there's no change."

The words felt like a replay of last year. No change. It was what I had expected, yet it still stung a little, I had really hoped that there had been some more improvement.

"Your EF is still stable at 60%, and your heart remains at 17% enlarged. There's no worsening, which is the important part," he continued, his tone reassuring.

I nodded, absorbing the information. It wasn't bad news, which was a victory in itself.

My heart wasn't getting worse, and that stability was what I had to hold onto. But, at the same time, I had secretly hoped for more. Hoped that maybe, just maybe, my heart would continue to heal beyond what seemed like a plateau.

He smiled, I think it is time to stop the medication, your heart has held steady at half dose, so we will stop your medication. I am happy for you to see your GP regularly and come back in twelve months. But if you get worried about anything make sure you talk to your GP.

It was the news we were hoping for, no more medication, however part of me wished for more, a clearer indication of progress, a sign that all my hard work, my lifestyle changes, we're paying off not just holding steady.

As we left the office, I had to remind myself of how far I had come. Two years ago, I had sat in the office facing a 3-year life expectancy, a dramatically enlarged heart, and my future had seemed uncertain. Now, I was living life again hopeful, running around after the kids, working, exercising doing all the things I thought I might have to give up, and was just about to stop all my heart medication.

There was no change, but sometimes, no change was exactly the news you needed to hear. For now, I could live my life knowing that stability was its own kind of victory.

August 2024

I am not typically an anxious person, but every time I walk into my cardiologist's office and sit there waiting for the results of the echocardiogram, I can feel my heart start to race. It's an odd irony, the very thing I'm here to monitor suddenly feels out of control. My blood pressure rises, and a slight tension settles over me, no matter how hard I try to stay calm.

The weight of what's at stake is never lost on me. If that first heart operation hadn't been successful, I might not even be sitting here today, my three year initial life expectancy number has been and gone, I would now be in the bonus territory. That thought alone sends a wave of mixed emotions through me, gratitude, fear, and a bit of disbelief. I made it through the worst, but what if there's something new lurking beneath the surface this time?

Even though I've been in this seat so many times before, and the results over the past two years have all been steady, there's always that underlying tension. Was my body more reliant on the medicine than I realised, and had twelve months of the medication left a mark.

After all, it's my heart. You can't see what's happening inside you, and that unknown is what makes it so unsettling. The heart is so vital, yet so mysterious. You don't always feel it when things are going wrong, and that's what makes waiting for these results so nerve-wracking. I've heard the reassuring words from my doctor time and time again, "You're stable," "Everything's holding steady," but the fear of what *could* be there is always just beneath the surface.

I take a deep breath and try to settle myself, reminding myself of how far I've come since the diagnosis, how my heart has healed. But still, there's something about the heart, its fragility, its importance, that always brings this moment to a heightened intensity. I sit, waiting for the doctor to walk in, hoping for the best but preparing myself for whatever news is to come. I look towards Scott so thankful that he has been able to be with me every step of the way, but also aware that both of us have our own journey through this diagnosis.

As the cardiologist walked in, I sat up a little straighter, my palms felt clammy against the cool leather chair. My eyes dart between the doctor and Scott as I prepare myself for the routine I had become so familiar with, heart rate checks, measurements, and a discussion of my progress. He glanced over the latest echocardiogram results, and I felt my heart pick up speed, just like it always did at these appointments. I thought back to the day of my first diagnosis, the numbing shock of hearing that I could only have three years to live. I remembered counting every heart beat, daily checks of my stats on my watch. I had come so far, but back in this room took my right back to that day, that feeling of helplessness.

After a moment, he looked up with a smile. "Well, the good news is, everything is stable. Your heart is strong, and although there's been no further improvement, it's holding steady. The enlargement is still at 17%, but it hasn't worsened, which is a positive sign."

His words sank in slowly. Stable I had spent so long obsessing over every heartbeat, every potential sign that things were either improving or getting worse. But now, he was telling me I was okay, not perfect, but okay. And I realised that was enough. Stability itself was a gift.

"You don't need to come back for another two years, it's time to get back to normal." he continued.

I smiled, a sense of relief washing over me. Two years until my next appointment. It felt like a lifetime compared to the constant check-ins I had grown used to. I wasn't entirely out of the woods, but the fact that my heart had remained stable for so long was a victory in itself.

As we left the office, past the other patients concern etched on their faces, and outside into the bright sunshine, and fresh air, I felt lighter, I was finally free from the constant worry that had hung over me for years. My heart, though not perfect, was strong enough to keep me moving forward. I could live my life with fewer restrictions, no more daily reminders of looming danger. We could look forward to the future without the constant worry about feeling like my heart was on a countdown, that I couldn't escape. I was officially in the clear.

Facing Your Mortality

The cliche that facing your mortality makes you appreciate all you have is even more profound that it first seems. When I first sat in my cardiologist office, being told that I faced a life expectancy of three to five years, I didn't have time to process it, I was overwhelmed. I threw myself into action, Taking the medication, changing my diet, giving up all caffeine, having the operation, and staying strong for my family. It was purely survival mode, keeping calm so our children wouldn't know the gravity of the situation. However, as the years went on and my heart become stable, I began to have a bit more time to reflect and process how it has changed me.

Whether it is just me and the way that I process things, or the role I play as a mother, but this busyness of life allowed me to carry on, especially in the early days of the diagnosis before we knew the operation had worked. Others around would get triggered when we watched movies or TV shows where a parent passed away or had a heart condition, with many shows turned off prematurely but I was able to compartmentalise and keep pushing through. I never allowed myself to sit in the diagnosis I had things to do, dreams to pursue.

When confronted with the fragility of life, I found it bought so many more things into focus, the things that really matter to me. Creating memories with my husband and children. Cherishing the little things, the little moments that matter; the morning hugs from my kids, fun loud and chaotic singalongs to musicals in the car, jumping in the photos with the kids, not just taking them. Fewer things and more experiences. For me it has always been important to create memories with my children, ensuring their childhood was something they cherished. Ensuring that no matter what they would no they are loved and valued.

The shift in perspective also meant saying yes to my dreams. Publishing my first children's book, something I had always wanted to do, but I had let life get in the way. It was not just about publishing the book, but also about leaving a lasting legacy for my children. I think about families sitting around at bedtime, reading something I created, and creating memories with their own children with something I wrote is truly inspiring and humbling. In turn writing this book about how the experience has changed me is another part of my journey, but for others it might be a different personal project, a different dream that they want to see fulfilled.

Facing my own mortality also made me realise that I have spent two many years living consumed by my own insecurities, worried about what everyone else would think of me. I embraced colour in my wardrobe, no more hiding behind dark clothes, instead embracing life. I swapped the black and greys that have been my way of hiding for years, with blues, greens and reds. It's a reminder that my body is so much more than just a number on a scale, it is the very reason that I am still here.

When you start taking medication and have to stop exercising the weight begins to pile on, and in the past I would let that consume me, but I have a knew found respect for my body. I know that for me know that I have been cleared to exercise again, its time to change again, I have been given a second chance, and I need to give my body the respect it deserves. I am committed to building my strength, not to chase an ideal, but instead each workout is a reminder that my heart is beating strong.

Ultimately the journey has taught me to live with intention, live with purpose, and to prioritise what matters most to me my Family. I don't just plan our days anymore, I plan them with purpose. I want our children to know they should love fiercely, pursue their dreams, and life life to the fullest.

Whilst I still wish that I did not have to live with Cardiomyopathy, I still live with the motto 'No regrets'.

The Journey

We sat at the table, waiting for our meal, the weight of the news settling in. The results were amazing, better than I had dared to hope that Summer day when I had walked into the hospital, waiting for the cardiologist skilled hands to perform the ablation.

Yet, I was surprised, instead of feeling joy or elation, instead I felt numb. It was hard to grasp that if the operation hadn't been a success I wouldn't be sitting there sharing in this moment with my husband. The reality of that moment left me feeling both humble and surreal, as if I was watching my life from a distance, seeing just how different my families life could have been if it hadn't worked.

I had just been given the amazing news that my life was returning to normal, I wouldn't have to return to the cardiologist for two years, the constant stress, worry that had become part of our life was finally lifting. However it didn't feel real. I kept waiting for something to sink in, for the joy to really hit. There is a strange gap between what I was told, and the cloud I had been living under for the last three and a half years.

It was amazing to think that this journey all started four years early with a random comment about a 'missed heartbeat' and now finally four years later, we were sitting here, a new chapter beginning, the long journey over.

The Journey had not been easy, however it has taught me to cherish every moment, listen to every niggle, big and small, and to embrace the lessons, the challenges that life throws at you. I had learned to understand and appreciate life so much more, that even through the unpredictability of it.

As I once again glanced down at my apple watch on my wrist, that watch that had been my early warning sign that something was wrong. I cant help but feel a profound sense of gratitude to the innovators of the world.

The innovators in technology, that built something that alerted me to a danger before I even knew it was there, The innovators in medication, in surgery, that created medication, and operations that would fix and repair the damage it reminds me how the watch on my arm is a symbol of so much more to me now.

The watch that once seemed like a fun gadget on my wrist to play music or check messages, has become a symbol of survival and resilience.

The watch was now a constant reminder of how precious and fragile life is. Every time I check the time, read a notification, or look at my step count, I remember how;

The Apple watch saved my life.

Thanks for Reading!

I hope you enjoyed this book as much as I loved creating it! Your support means the world to me, and I'd love to hear your thoughts or see how the story inspired you.

You can connect with me on social media or via my website, or write my a review on amazon:

Feel free to share your favorite moments, ask questions, or just say hello. Don't forget to tag me—I'd love to see your posts!

Instagram: sarahmcphersonauthor
Facebook: Sarah McPherson Author
tiktok: sarahmcphersonauthor

If you'd like to stay up-to-date on new releases, book events, or behind-the-scenes news, sign up for my newsletter at **sarahmcphersonauthor.com.au**.

Thank you for being part of this journey!

Warm wishes,

Sarah McPherson

www.ingramcontent.com/pod-product-compliance
Lightning Source LLC
Chambersburg PA
CBHW022057290426
44109CB00014B/1136